the shoe shine parlor

poems et al

The Bronx Trilogy by w r rodriguez

Print Editions
the shoe shine parlor poems et al. Ghost Pony Press, 1984.
concrete pastures of the beautiful bronx. Zeugpress, 2008.
from the banks of brook avenue. Zeugpress, 2016.

Electronic Editions
the shoe shine parlor poems et al. Zeugpress: Smashwords Edition, 2014.
concrete pastures of the beautiful bronx. Zeugpress: Smashwords Edition, 2014.
from the banks of brook avenue. Zeugpress: Smashwords Edition, 2015.

the shoe shine parlor

poems et al

second edition

w r rodriguez

═══════ zeugpress ═══════

Grateful appreciation to the Mary Roberts Rinehart Foundation for supporting the completion of the original manuscript.

And thanks to Robert Stern for his friendship over the years.

The first edition of *the shoe shine parlor poems et al* was published by Ghost Pony Press in 1984.

> **Acknowledgments:**
>
> Poems from this book appeared in the following magazines and anthologies:
>
> *Abraxas, Bronx Accent: A Literary and Pictorial History of the Bronx; Collage of 9 & 1; The Croton Review; Editor's Choice III: Fiction, Poetry & Art from the U.S. Small Press (1984-1990); Epoch; Fistflowers: Poems of Struggle and Revolution; I didn't know there were Latinos in Wisconsin I; I didn't know there were Latinos in Wisconsin II;* and *The U.S. Latino Review.*

Second Edition

© 1984, 2016 w r rodriguez
All rights reserved

Printed in the United States of America

ISBN 978-0-9632201-4-1

zeugpress

Contents

Preface to the Second Edition of *the shoe shine parlor poems et al* vii

I
the shoe shine parlor poems

making it 11
the cop 12
the shoe shine poem 13
al's pictures of old times 14
grandfather 16
coffee 17
blinky 18
the banana man 20
little spic & big man 21
the bust 24
jim 25
the long walk to bed 26
private rivers 27

II
et al

the moon does not linger 31
Something Fishy 32
the miracle 34
the old woman 35
late one hot august 36
the day i threw thoreau off the roof 37
they disappear 38
of bootblacks 40
what i remember most about hughes avenue 41
the accordion player 42
butch 44
weeds 46
the bronx at the end of the mind 47

Bibliography: Previous Publications 48

dedicated to my parents and to my wife

Preface to the Second Edition of *the shoe shine parlor poems et al*

This book is dedicated to my parents and to my wife, and rightly so. My mother liked to talk, and passed on family stories, in elaborate detail, to me and to a variety of cousins. My father, whose family suffered through the Great Depression, and who worked his way up from office clerk to office manager, did nothing to stop me from avoiding a career in banking, or from foregoing engineering and declaring myself an English major. My wife does not define happiness and fulfillment in terms of money. If she did, she probably would not have married someone who wanted to write poetry.

Without assimilating my mother's sense of detail, I do not know if I could write the way I do. Without my father's tolerance of my youthful decisions, I might never have become a teacher of high school English, which allowed me to pay the bills while pursuing my interests in literature and writing. And my wife, going to poetry readings and reading revisions of my work, has been my best emotional support and editorial guide over many years.

I wrote the first poem, "making it," in a Bronx laundromat. I was in college and living at home. Watching the family laundry spin around seems an appropriate context for the poem's inspiration. When I moved to Wisconsin, I began writing "the cop," "blinky," "the bust," and "jim." Like most of my work, they are based on true stories, but I often change the names of the leading characters. I was influenced by the Beats and by the Romantics, and it occurred to me that The Bronx was a worthy subject for poetry.

Among the first in my family to attend college, I had moved from the tenements of The Bronx to attend graduate school at the University of Wisconsin-Madison. Having started my career as a bootblack, I was somehow fulfilling the Great American Dream. It seemed fitting to call my first book *the shoe shine parlor poems et al.*

The cover photograph, taken in about 1929, shows my aunt, my grandfather, three uncles (two biological, one adopted) and several customers. After the riots of the 1960's, the glass windows were replaced with plexiglass portholes bolted into plywood. By the 1970's, sneakers, sandals, and vinyl shoes made their impact, and the shoe shine parlor's income declined.

My uncle recruited me into the family business when I was eleven. I began by washing the shoes. After several months I was entrusted with completing the entire shine. Shining shoes is often looked down on in America. But it is an honest job. One works hard, sees the results of his labor, and is paid and given a tip. I was proud of being a bootblack. I built muscle, learned to interact with people, and used my savings to pay my share of college tuition. And I got to learn what was going on in the neighborhood without being directly involved.

So being a bootblack, and listening to my mother, and having a tolerant father, and an understanding wife (who also grew up in the South Bronx and who also was an English major) enabled me to write this book. I am indebted to these blessings, and also to Ingrid Swanberg, whose Ghost Pony Press published the first edition of *the shoe shine parlor poems et al* in 1984.

Much has happened in the decades since the first appearance of this book. My parents have passed. My children have grown and moved on. The Bronx has been rebuilt. I retired from teaching, but three decades of producing a high school literary magazine taught me how to do layout and gave me some practice in editing. In 2008, I spent the summer learning how to use a new layout program. I did this by producing the sequel to *the shoe shine parlor poems*. I entitled it *the concrete pastures of the beautiful bronx*, and published it under my Zeugpress imprint. I decided then that I wanted to complete a trilogy of books about The Bronx and the urban experience. The third book, *from the banks of brook avenue*, is being released in 2016. My wife has been very gracious in reading and commenting on numerous revisions of the poems.

As the trilogy is completed, I am reprinting a limited number of copies of *the shoe shine parlor poems et al*. Though my work has evolved over the decades, I remain pleased with this book, and the text is the same as that of the first edition. I simply want to have enough copies to complement *the concrete pastures of the beautiful bronx* and *from the banks of brook avenue* when I offer *the bronx trilogy* to my readers.

I remain most grateful to Ingrid and to Ghost Pony Press and to all those who have supported and influenced my work over the years.

w r rodriguez
January, 2016

I

the shoe shine parlor poems

making it

great grandfather burned some government office
in some spanish town   made it to puerto rico
hiding in jungles   huts   from wanted posters
& police   must've hid pretty well because

somehow grandfather made it to new york
rolling cigars   surviving the depression   & me
putting dirt in his pipe   sitting always
by the television   watching yankee games
never cheering   smiling sometimes
dying in a railway flat
on cypress avenue where he lived twenty years
in the south bronx

where my mother also lived   forty years
met my father   married   sent him to wall street
each day dressed in the suit he wore
even on saturdays

while she stayed home
remembering to me her father   the handsome
little italian   who also made it to philadelphia
then to new york   the south bronx   sweeping speakeasies
founding the family business

                                        the shoe shine parlor
i worked there seven years   sweating
reading plato's symposium   tristram shandy
playboy magazines between shines
not speaking spanish or italian but laughing anyway
at the customers' dirty jokes

                                      never listening
even if they spoke english   mind never there
body pushing brushes   burning two-&-a-half-cent cigars
mind someplace else   in riverdale   la rive gauche
in bed with the playmate of the month
in that spanish town a hundred years ago
but always

someplace else

the cop

one week he was a movie star
dyed his hair blond   quite unusual
for a puerto rican   & he strolled
up & down 138th street   smiled
gave autographs   & occasionally
a 3×5 glossy

suddenly he was a cop   the only one
i ever saw walk a beat in our neighborhood
138th & 137th   brook avenue   saint ann's
even brown place   in a regulation blue uniform
shoes shined   night stick twirling   a tin badge
& cap guns in a cowboy holster

every night he guarded the newsstand till it closed
got a free paper   & walked the newsman home
saturday afternoons the children followed him
the men who sat on milk boxes   playing dominoes
drinking beer   talking about the cock fights
would yell   *hey officer*   & ask directions
to places they were not going
or tell him of cars double parked around the corner

but he was a nice cop   gave accurate directions
did not give tickets
& when the streetlights went out   he directed traffic

when the riots came   in the summer of 67
or 68   probably both   he was there
in the middle of 138th street   with a riot helmet
& his dime store guns   with five or six
hundred other cops   who chased the crowds up the block
or were chased   or who stood in doorways
watching the stores   dodging bricks   while he sat
on a friend's car so it would not be overturned

once in a while someone would shout
rotten pig   & throw bottles at him
but they were always aimed to land
ten or twenty feet away
& i never saw a cop   smile
so much in a riot

the shoe shine poem

i tell ya man
i finished the shine
& as he got off the stand
i saw a gun in his belt

i started praying
as he reached for his wallet

then he gave me
a buck
& told me to keep the change
& i said to myself

my prayers are answered

i ain't had a buck shine in a month

al's pictures of old times

a boxer doing an l sullivan pose
three men in two piece bathing suits drinking beer
our shoe shine parlor back in the '20s
when there were stands outside too
& uncle giaco was there
& grandpa
funny calling him grandpa
because i never met him

& i don't remember giaco
except ma would tell me
how skippy howled every midnight
for six months after the car
killed him

he wasn't really our uncle though
my grandparents took him in
when he was just off the boat
& he became a relative
worked in the parlor with al
opened up every morning at six
washed down the marble stand
& polished the brass footrests
six or seven days a week

went back to italy once
a month after his mother's funeral
but mussolini wanted to draft him
he had been a runner for general pershing
& that was war enough for him
so he stayed on the ship
came back to brook avenue
& years later was run over by a car
crossing 138th street to buy us ice cream

& snapshots of faces i didn't know
but al remembered
one or two of them gangsters
in the '30s they would sit on the stand

& polish their guns
al said
while he shined their shoes

photos of cats & dogs & cousins
a drill sergeant & some cops
aunts & uncles
old christmasses & customers
all turning yellow
behind the dusty glass

grandfather

his father was an exporter
so it wasn't as hard for him to leave italy
as it was for a lot of others   & work
his way up the coast   florida to phillie
bought land there with his brothers-in-law
had a barber shop   & a store   on main street too
but he left it   all in a family argument
returned only for funerals   & weddings
the old fashioned kind   with buffets   home pressed wine
virgin brides

he made it to new york   with his wife
& the children they had on the boat   & in various other states
then in manhattan my   mother   the ninth & last
not counting the two who died of pneumonia & tb
all living in a cold water flat by the polo grounds
then in the south bronx   right around the corner
from the shoe shine parlor he bought
in the early '20s

               worked it with his sons
swept streets   & speakeasies on the side
bartended after the repeal   had as much fun
as anyone during the depression   went fishing & crabbing
in pelham bay before it was polluted   & sometimes
on sundays   treated ma to a ride on the third avenue el
& once a year   took the whole family for a picnic
sailing the dayliner to bear mountain

               but mostly he worked
ten or twelve hours a day   came home   took a short nap
woke   went for a walk   returned with the paper
read it & made sure his daughters were home by nine

he never let his children curse   & never
let anyone call him a son of a bitch
would say   *i've got a real mother*   & fight to prove it
only time he'd ever fight   & he usually won
once he even got hit over the head with a barstool
but he proved he had a real mother anyway

two days later   he collapsed behind the bar
his friends   carried his corpse
home   in a chair

coffee

a small man with a twisted body
five feet three
a size six shoe
& the other a four
so it wasn't much trouble
to give him a free shine
while he spoke to al

not really talk
but al understood his
choked sounds & gestures
& understood almost everybody
no matter what language they spoke
or smiled & pretended to

we helped coffee on & off the stand
when he came around on saturday afternoons
or sunday mornings after church

he usually brought al coffee
sometimes smelled of whiskey

& was always happy

blinky

had a glass eye that didn't fit well
but he was too poor to get another
so folks called him blinky   the one eyed junkie
because he was a junkie   & twitched a lot
trying to keep his eye from falling out

he wasn't like the other junkies who weren't like him
& who hung around   wasted   waiting to score
watching who to rob   & mugging people
angel's father's head bloodied   stabbed in the chest too
not because he fought back   but because they wouldn't take chances
or waste time asking   & in a rush they pushed maria
who lived next door & was seventy six years old
down the stairs   took her pocketbook   the social security money
just enough to pay the rent   & buy thirty dollars food each month
she spent ten weeks in the hospital   with fractured ribs
& a broken hip   so they could get their fix
but blinky wasn't like them

maybe he didn't have much of a habit to support
or maybe he dealt on the side
but he'd just hang around the supermarket
carry packages home for a quarter or half-a-buck
take odd jobs   paint apartments
sweep sidewalks   bring down the garbage for the super
in bad times he'd beg by the subway

one night blinky overdosed in some basement
folks said he didn't move an eyelid
when the cops carried him to the ambulance

word got around he was dead
someone painted a cross on the sidewalk
put a bouquet of plastic flowers next to a hat
read the bible & took a collection   *for blinky's funeral*
he said   & the old women walking home from the stores
dropped in dimes & quarters
some stopped to listen to the prayers

two weeks later blinky returned
he woke up in lincoln hospital   stole some clothes & walked out
right past the cops & nurses   back to 138th street hoping for a fix

when he saw the cross still painted on the sidewalk
& found out about our donations
he had some fine ideas on spending the money
so he & a few friends went looking for the man who took the collection

but no one could ever find him

the banana man

looked like jimmy durante
had a room on 139th street
worked for d loi & sons
trucking bananas all over new york

got a free shine every saturday
gave us a huge bag of bananas
talked a while about the flats & trots
then took the bus to belmont or the big a

worked all the overtime he could
saved his money
& spent his vacations at saratoga

little spic & big man

little spic
the name he was known by   but a person
could only speak it with affection   little spic
wasn't shorter or taller   or bigger & meaner
or cooler & mellower than anyone else
& he didn't try to be

                              he just held his own
through tough times   struck hard   ran fast
when he had to   now he was the old timer
of the block   & drove the smoothest bus
in the bronx   *too old to turn from anything*
he joked with the passengers

                            & no taxi
ever beat him in a fair race   he knew enough
of the ways of the world to negotiate
translate or otherwise assist a friend in need
through any crisis from a wedding or a funeral
to football tickets & the recovery of stolen or confiscated property

he had many friends   never sought enemies
earned his title in grammar school during the '20s
when the irish & italian & german kids who ruled the streets back then
would rough him up & get him down   until one day
he grabbed the biggest guy by the collar
shook his head a few times & said   in a fierce voice   *yeah*

i'm little spic   so what of it   that bunch
never troubled him again   they became buddies
& stuck up for each other like brothers
they were as tough as they had to be to survive
& as lucky   they lived according to the code of their pride
never crossed a friend   never struck from behind

or without good reason   they never took nothing
from those who had nothing   & that was more than could be said
for the loan sharks   local politicos   & insurance agents
who sold bogus policies   promises   & quicksand loans
to depression families   *it's a hard life*
people are strange   little spic thought

& no matter how many friends he might make
he knew that some folks would always   if only
in a small but certain way   think of him as just
a little spic   so he figured he'd get the jump on them
any way he could   no friend of his
ever used his christian name again

                              & during the depths
of the '30s his drinking buddies passed him a good tip
about a rough job   & they worked together until the war
driving trucks in the garment district   which is where
they learned the old trick of carrying a lead pipe in a rolled up newspaper
to fight off hijackers

                     & thirty years later
when he walked home late that friday night from the bus route
he got in '47   he had a foot long rod of bicycle frame
in an evening news to fend off muggers   & so when big man
who was not so big he didn't have to prove his muscle
& who was known to prefer the pleasure of assault & battery

to the profits of pure thievery   staggered up to little spic
& grabbed his throat yelling   *you damn ricans*
i'm gonna kill allaya   & bury you in jersey   little spic
afraid it might be the last thing he'd ever do
swung his newspaper with all his might   & walked away with no hurry
leaving big man unconscious on the sidewalk

but he didn't get too far when a police car drove up
& one of the cops yelled   *hey old man*
what happened to that big guy over there
& little spic said   with no hesitation
i don't know   he was walking around real drunk
& he just collapsed

& the other cop yelled to two young guys
who were sipping a pint in a doorway across the street
hey what happened to that big guy over there
& they answered with no hesitation
he was walking around real drunk   said one
he just collapsed   said the other

well that's as good as any place to sleep it off
muttered the cop at the wheel as they drove away

& little spic walked home to the wife who always waited up for him
& the two guys kept sipping their pint until all was clear
then they crossed the deserted street & walked up
real quiet

                     to big man who was snoring drunk on the sidewalk
nose up   jowls drooling   sprawled beside some trash cans
& boxes & bags of garbage   with a touch
light as a fly his wallet was lifted   he never woke
so holding their noses they stole his shoes
& biting back laughter threw them beneath a car

big man snored on in his stupor   so they slipped off his pants
threw them upon a nearby fire escape & split to spread the news
a hundred folks soon gathered   *let's take a good look*
at this strong mouthed giant who seems to have insulted one too many of us
for his own health   someone said loudly in spanish   & it was a sight
because big man wore no underwear that night

& it wasn't long till the laughter woke him   the crowd moved back
big man swayed to his feet & stretched a bit until he realized
he was standing surrounded in the street
so he reached to a pocket for his knife in case there was trouble
& jolted when he felt his bare skin
they're on the fire escape   yelled a little kid
big man ran to the fire escape as the crowd opened around him
he ain't so big   shrieked a woman from her window
& big man tried leaping to reach his pants   he couldn't jump too high
because of his hangover but he kept trying anyway
the crowd became hysterical   big man went berserk
& tackled some guy around the waist yelling   *give me your pants*

give me your pants   *give me your pants*   until three cops drove up
& grabbed him   but he got one in a bear hug still yelling
give me your pants   *give me your pants*   as more cops dragged him away

& even after he jumped bail he was never seen in these parts again
though his name was remembered in stories & drunken ballads
which in our neighborhood always ended with the moral

you don't mess around with little spic

the bust

i knew bo & bub   the two detectives who busted frank
they came in for a shine   drunk every friday night
never tipped   & seldom paid us   not like the other cops
not like the pimps & bookies who'd give bills
& say   *keep the change*

once bub told georgey   as he sat next to him on our stand
that they almost caught him stealing that mustang last night
& would get him the next   bust his ass too
but georgey laughed & said they wouldn't

& i sure wish i'd pounded   the brush into a corn or bunion
because frank never did nothing
except box in the golden gloves   train all day
walk his dog at night   & look a little
like georgey the rat king   who was doing lots of things

but it was frank they arrested   tackled him crossing 138th street
cuffed him & drove him down by the river
to the alley beside the furniture warehouse
where they beat him with blackjacks   held guns to his head & said
they'd shoot him & throw him in the harlem river

then they kicked frank & beat him with their pistols
until two patrol cars drove up to arrest them
but bo & bub identified themselves   so they all brought frank
to be booked with grand larceny   petty theft   resisting arrest
& several counts of assault & battery upon officers of the peace

the dog came home alone & frank's mother was worried
but a few neighbors ran in yelling   *frank's just been busted*
so they rushed to the police station
& sat there three hours before frank arrived
& even then the desk sergeant wouldn't let his mother see him
or send for a doctor   until some friends
got a manhattan lawyer to take the case   free of charge

now bo & bub shine their own shoes   they're doing two to five
frank's walking a little dizzy   he can't fight no more
& georgey the rat king   is still   doing lots of things

jim

i was thirteen   there wasn't much to do on those sticky august nights
except listen to the yanks drop two to the twins
look out the window   maybe see a star or two
& catch the latest on the all night outdoor poker game
when suddenly   thirty or forty guys turned the corner
from saint ann's avenue   came right down 138th street
ripping off car aerials   slashing tires
throwing bottles at a stray dog

the gamblers grabbed their beer & abandoned their milk boxes
as the gang hurled trash cans through store windows
set woolworth's on fire   carried off a few televisions
& strolled away laughing into the night

ten minutes later the cops & firemen arrived
people looked from their windows to see what had happened
& our super   old jim   was sweeping the gutter
when a cop walked up   & bashed his head with a night stick

maybe he thought old jim was one of the gang
& couldn't run fast enough to escape
or maybe he thought old jim pulled off the whole riot by himself
but i don't know because no one ever saw that cop again
& jim wasn't arrested   just taken to the hospital
& let out two weeks later with a bandaged head & a broken nose
& went right back to work   sweeping hallways & collecting the garbage

folks would see him & ask   *how you doing jim*
& tell him he should go to the civil liberties union
find out who that cop was   & sue him   sue the city too
but i knew jim wouldn't

                & he didn't
he was an old black gentleman   grew up in virginia
*when i was a boy   we couldn't walk on the sidewalk
if white folks was walking on it   had to walk in the gutter*
he told me one day while i shined his shoes

& now he just said   *i can't sue that cop
it wouldn't help my head none
besides   that cop is the law
i was brought up to obey the law
& i'm too old to change*

the long walk to bed

my footsteps echo down empty streets. the moon is full, but the stores are hidden behind steel roll down gates, & the shoe shine parlor is boarded over with plywood. the trash cans are in their usual places, & patches of black ice are unmoved by the wind. it does not snow much anymore, but the night is very damp, & cold. in my building, rusted icicles hang from the hallway radiator. they are a month old & still growing. i dream of nothing, shivering in my sleep, cold as a parking meter.

private rivers

private rivers
is dead   he stepped
on a mine   on the wrong road
in a mistaken land   in an old war   his young
dogtagged blood exploded   & dried brown upon green
backed leaves   that rotted in the chemical breeze

private rivers   is dead   he wound up
on the wrong road   the gossip goes
because the illiterate corporal   could not read the map
to the literate lieutenant who could not read maps
& was actually an actuary   & the old sergeant
had retired yesterday   & the new sergeant had not yet been delivered

& the platoon radio was not working
so the lieutenant   who never took advice from noncoms
could not consult the captain who had chronic gout & never left the base
& the major was on leave   & the general
at the peace talks   did not hear the explosion
but signed the letter anyway

the wake was a closed coffin   flag & flowers
affair   fat priests   babies bawling to be fed
nervous brothers   pale sisters   some pfc's
a corporal in a wheelchair   the grandmother
prayed & cried & shrieked her grief
& the widow fainted at the cemetery

private rivers is dead   the news spread
& shattered our neighborhood
he was a seventh son   never known
to be in the wrong place at the wrong time
or to leave a poker game empty handed   never robbed   never arrested
never beaten by a crazy cop   & he was always lucky

playing the numbers   until they drew him
a seven in the draft lottery   & now
everyone was nervous   the patriotic eulogy
no consolation   *how would life deal to us*
spoke up a drunk gambler
if it didn't leave enough of him to fill a coffin

II

et al

the moon does not linger

the moon does not linger
in this neighborhood

naked as a silver dollar
she sneaks out from behind a building
or a cloud of smoke

and hurries west
into the suburbs of new jersey
or the corporate farms of quiet kansas

leaving the poor lunatics
madly staggering
or dreaming amid constellations
of streetlights
counting
their fortune

Something Fishy

Be the first on your block!
the ad proclaims
Wear our new Prodigal Princess shoes!
    Clear plastic!
        Happily hyper-elevated!
            With gold buckles
and a real live goldfish in each heel!

Here she comes—
the first to obey the commanding black majuscules.
She smiles
    proud as a successful fisherman.
Like Ahab she limps
    bitten by the sharp gold buckles.

She sails across the street
buoyant on the real live goldfish
    whose reflection she watches
unaware of the red light
    and the speeding white bus
        now spouting its horn.

Full speed ahead
she escapes the thrashing king of rolling highways
    but her left shoe
        broken at the buckle
            does not.

The fish
    though constantly trying
cannot swim through the plastic
    until the heel is crushed.
Then he flies freely through the air
    graceful as a sea gull
        an albatross
            an erne.
He falls to the asphalt
    wiggles his tail in dead earnest
        and dies.

Lamenting the price of the shoes
cursing the bus

she hobbles on the surviving heel
and sinks into the crowd of shoppers.

The fish rests on his side.
One eye
     always open
          stares
               at the sky.

the miracle

jerry knelt outside the church. eric hid behind a pillar on the loggia. as an old woman walked by, jerry yelled: *oh god, please send me a pair of sneakers.* a slightly used pair of sneakers fell into jerry's waiting hands. the old woman's eyes opened wide. she was about to kneel when eric, barefoot, came down the stairs and smiled. the old woman raised her cane. jerry scrambled to his feet and began to run, but the old woman just shook her head and tapped her cane on the sidewalk. and laughed.

the old woman

through the window the world hangs
painted shut long ago
brown
with grease and dust
a lifetime of his smoke
and her cooking with garlic

the great
great grandmother sews
in time to the clock's ticking
stitches which hold
everything together

the empty birdcage shivers in a draft
his pipe cold upon the ashtray

she draws her shawl
embroidered with canaries
and flowers

children playing in the distance
her fingers
are nimble
still

late one hot august

late one august
so hot and sticky it seemed
september would never come
late one hot august
in the fireplug's frigid spray
a girl splashed naked and young

late one hot august
while a clutched beercan cooled the hydrant's roar to a hiss
and rainbows bubbled over cobblestones
late one hot august
a fountain arched silver to the sky
and fell

late one hot august
when numb fingers let the bent can slip
and sprawling the child flung far into the street
late one hot august
a passing coal truck
crushed her head like an eggshell
late one hot august
her unborn life ran out
late one hot august
and rippled with the currents
late one hot august
and sank into the sewers
late one hot august
of brook avenue

the day i threw thoreau off the roof

was three days after a riot, was two days after our mayor toured the property damage, was a day after the radio told me i lived in a slum, was my first day off work in months. the day i threw thoreau off the roof, was a hot day which melted the tar, was another day of the mosquitoes which bred in the backwater of the sewer our city would never fix and bit anything that could still bleed. the day i threw thoreau off the roof, was the angry day i refused to do my homework, was the happy day i watched yellow pages flutter down the airshaft like poisoned pigeons. the day i threw thoreau off the roof, was not up to civil disobedience, was just sick of reading about those damn beans.

they disappear

day and night they disappear
lovers of smiles and moonlight and swollen dolphin bellies
that shoot like stars over the waves
whispering
a birth
a birth

they disappear
some beaten on side streets in the afternoon
while the children are in school studying history
some dragged screaming from their lovers' arms
before the newborn moon can open its eye

they disappear
are hidden underground where there is no green utopia
are left to slow death in the gray world
are chained naked to dank walls and nibbled by desperate rats
are denied the tomb's comforts

they disappear
although some are allowed to return after many years
with beards and volumes which are read and reviewed
sold underground or catalogued in the library of congress
although some organize rape workshops
some fight for the poor
and some whose constitutions permit it preach
in parks to squirrels and pigeons

they disappear
no
grendel the great fen monster has not eaten them
no
singing fairies have not carried them away
no

hands with knives and guns and government papers
are taking them
hands with blackjacks and chains and cattle prodders
are taking them
hands shaped like fists
are taking them

voices of many languages
condemn them
curses in barrooms and on bronx streets
condemn them
military juntas and corporate conspiracies and terrorist kidnappings
condemn them
condemn them
condemn them
and they disappear

soon
there will be no one left

of bootblacks *(for al)*

the eyes of bootblacks
do not see where shoes go
after they walk out of sight

the foreheads of bootblacks
recall the hides' stains
and soles worn beneath the buff

the hair of bootblacks
is every color
their backs droop with the growing strength of age

the arms of bootblacks
snap the rag's rhythm as hours dance
their feet seldom travel
yet are weary with the day's journey

the mouths of bootblacks
tell no lies
and speak the world's tales

the ears of bootblacks
hear all within earshot
even when they do not listen

the hands of bootblacks
are calloused where brush joins flesh

their art is to pound
the grin of a thunderbolt
onto a landscape of bunion
and crease

what i remember most about hughes avenue

where retired italians sweating in beach chairs
watch tides that never come

what i remember most

and midnight's nomads drift through the christmas wind

what i remember

that torrid apartment with walls of ice

what

is moments of twilight with you in my arms
a candle dancing upon a ceiling

there is joy among our shadows

we are lulled
to the flickering

and we
for
get

the accordion player

he is gone   that gray haired man
with the roman nose   who bellowed up airshaft
and alley   down street and avenue
songs the old folks knew   and danced
and seemed young forever in the immortality of music

he is gone   that arm swaying man
who tipped a gray cap   who smiled and skipped
fingered and squeezed the air
as if a virgin   who bed the wind in a box
as a loud deity

he is gone   who panned the gray windows
and ears of this iron city like a god   embarked
from the foothills of a golden time   shedding wordless ditties
that rustle migrant memory to a younger day
an older way   and the children were happy

silver   nickel   copper   pure from the outstretched arms
of the barely poor   too heavy with work
too thin with youth   to pump music from the grind and drone
the clatter and chatter of the trolley shaken cobblestones
and the crescent white belly through the orchard street suit   bulges

earns a mortal living   while crowds gather in groves
on hot streets   squinting   stunned after the gloom
of hallway and bedroom   the fruits of labor
ringing and clinging through the applause
rolling round the thick soled shuffle of his feet

or they stare   obscure paintings behind windowpanes
crooked in their frames   lining the long thoroughfares
and the stagnant airshafts   those interior courtyards
four walls of splotched mortar and rough cut brick
the cracked pavement below   a square of sky above

and the weatherbeaten clotheslines of the crisscrossed world between
drooping diapers and bedsheets that cry   underwear
dripping clean from the sweat of love   or they lean
from the worn sills of endless edifices   brown or maroon   ash or cream
crumbling crockets long rooted in brick   grave with the unique venations
    of life

a husband   a wife   baby in a bib   wrinkled women in grease
        bellied frocks
yank open the venetian blinds   plaid skirted high school girls
fondling lockets and dime store pearls   unshirted men   tattoos
and cigars   crucifixes   garlic cloves   a few scars
and everywhere the eyes of children

watch notes and chords rise   leaves on the updraft of a wild dream
burst from bustling esplanade and shaded yard   past corniced facades
where sparrows nest among the lotus and rosette of the festooned modillion
past spires and crenelations and the common copings of tile and stone
past patched tarpaper rooves and pigeons circling endlessly home

he is gone   that gay eyed man with the baggy clothes whom no spring
will ever return   who shuffled away while the sun swooped low
a breeze blew up the street   and the verdure burned with autumn
he is gone   into the miasmas of music   gone

butch

in darkness before the bronx sunrise when the fighting does end
    when the screaming side streets die down to damp silence
    when shattered glass embeds itself in dull memory

when sticks no longer swing   when the knife's flash
    no longer sparkles the guttural and shrieks of rabid snarling men
    and hysterical women   and illuminates the laughter
    and cries of wide eyed children

in darkness when bullets lie cold in graves of flesh and brick

in darkness when time is too quiet   he sets it right
and his cry echoes down the night
btchooooooooooooooooooooooooooooooooooooooooooooooooooooooo
btchooooooooooooooooooooooooooooooooooooooooooooooooooooooo

in darkness between the two suns and after fortune takes its daily toll
    after winners and losers shuffle home from curbside poker games
    that spiralled like a chant from sunset   long into the late night

after the midnight stickball champs share their last beer
    after the ivory dominoes are polished with a white cloth
    and entombed in black leather   after the crapshooters' prayers
    and dances roll to a death rattle   and the clicks
    and mutterings bury themselves in catacombs of tenements

in darkness when the gambling is done the clawed cock's feathers
    rise from the corpse in the wind

in darkness when time is too quiet   he sets it right
and his cry echoes down the night
btchooooooooooooooooooooooooooooooooooooooooooooooooooooooo
btchooooooooooooooooooooooooooooooooooooooooooooooooooooooo

in darkness between time's snake eyes dawns the dim light
    of forgotten childhood's crystalline afternoons
    before the gypsy cab strikes   before fresh blood
    casts like prophecy over iridescent asphalt   and the mind's shell
    cracks upon the squared sidewalks of concrete reality

    dawns the din of young afternoons   shouts of red rover
        red-light-green-light-1-2-3   skullcap   skullcap   skullcap
        running the hot streets   before brainsurgeons aping mortality
    drive metal plates like the cadillacs of civilization
    into the sprawling alleys of the run down psyche
    and the unfortunate soul is rescued from heavenly high rises
    which shine amid eternal streetlights
    beyond the wheelings and dealings of the stars

in darkness the urchins' sunny jeers
in darkness the lips refuse to close

in darkness when time is too quiet   he sets it right
and his cry echoes down the night
btchoooooooooooooooooooooooooooooooooooooooooooooooooooooooo
btchoooooooooooooooooooooooooooooooooooooooooooooooooooooooo

in darkness   in the crevice between two moments
    before the cock crows   before a trace of twilight
    fades the unseen east   after the starry pitch
    stained to the depths the night   and the moans
    of distant lovers strangled in sleep

when i stare into my own restless darkness

a silhouette in an unlit window
    a burning voice
               that certain eye
                            through the night
btchoooooooooooooooooooooooooooooooooooooooooooooooooooooooo
btchoooooooooooooooooooooooooooooooooooooooooooooooooooooooo

weeds

we are weeds

we are everywhere weeds who stand together and grow in lonely places
    where grass and trees will not

we are ancient weeds who have multiplied and sent our children
    upon the four winds to the polar wastelands and to the jungles
    and deserts of the great solar circle

we are strong weeds sweating at dawn   sick weeds choking on pesticides
    toiling weeds who grasp the rich earth   brittle weeds who wither
    beneath dry suns

we are wise weeds who fear bulldozers

we are sad weeds who watch cities rise like tombstones from the graves
    of our ancestors

we are many weeds who litter the lots of abandoned landlords   who loiter
    upon the renovated window boxes of graffitied brownstones

we are penniless weeds deposited along broken riverbanks where the corporate
    surplus flows to the ocean's vault

we are swaying weeds who crawl around factories   who are contaminated
    at industrial parks   erased in college campuses   and burnt upon
    suburban lawns

we are lofty weeds stranded on rooftop islands of soot   reckless weeds
    whistling between railroad ties as trains pass   carefree weeds
    in the city's eroded parks   dancing

we are restless weeds who creep through the concrete's cracks like banshees
    from the green underworld   who wail the foreclosed land where all share
    the earth's poverty   who moan in the wind   who bask in the sun
    who eat the soil   who drink the rain

we are weeds

we dream of freedom

the bronx at the end of the mind

each day clutching
on steeple and sill
of factory and office

the soot grows black

fire escapes rust
subways roar   rocking foundations
cracks in the pavement
flow wide   fast   free
and empty
into the gnarled tides
which gnash the cement shores
of this god trusting land

the stench that crawls from the sludge
wanders like a swart thought
through this harbor city

night calls the ghosts of spice
fried fish and incense
to dance out the windows

again the feast

our singing drowns the sea

Bibliography: Previous Publications

the accordion player
Editor's Choice III: Fiction, Poetry & Art from the U.S. Small Press (1984-1990). The Spirit That Moves Us Press. 1992.

blinky (selected lines)
Bronx Accent: A Literary and Pictorial History of the Bronx. Rutgers University Press. 2000.

the cop
I didn't know there were Latinos in Wisconsin: An Anthology of Hispanic Poetry. Friends of the Hispanic Community. 1989.
Fistflowers: Poems of Struggle and Revolution. (An anthology for the University of Wisconsin-Whitewater's Spring Poetry Festival.) 1988.
Epoch. Vol. 26, no.3, spring, 1977.

the day i threw thoreau off the roof
I didn't know there were Latinos in Wisconsin: 30 Hispanic Writers Volume II. Focus Communications. 1999.

grandfather (selected lines)
Bronx Accent: A Literary and Pictorial History of the Bronx. Rutgers University Press. 2000.

little spic & big man
I didn't know there were Latinos in Wisconsin: An Anthology of Hispanic Poetry. Friends of the Hispanic Community. 1989.
Fistflowers: Poems of Struggle and Revolution. (An anthology for the University of Wisconsin-Whitewater's Spring Poetry Festival.) 1988.
Abraxas. Vol. 27/28, 1983.

making it
Collage of 9 & 1. The Bronx Council on the Arts Inc. 1973.

the moon does not linger.
Croton Review. Vol. 1, no. 3, 1980.

private rivers
I didn't know there were Latinos in Wisconsin: An Anthology of Hispanic Poetry. Friends of the Hispanic Community. 1989.
Fistflowers: Poems of Struggle and Revolution. (An anthology for the University of Wisconsin-Whitewater's Spring Poetry Festival.) 1988.

they disappear
I didn't know there were Latinos in Wisconsin: An Anthology of Hispanic Poetry. Friends of the Hispanic Community. 1989.

weeds
The U.S. Latino Review. Issue 1, winter-spring 2000.

www.ingramcontent.com/pod-product-compliance
Lightning Source LLC
Chambersburg PA
CBHW031207160426
43193CB00008B/537